Comput

A Pocket Guide

Computer Forensics

A Pocket Guide

NATHAN CLARKE

IT Governance Publishing

Every possible effort has been made to ensure that the information contained in this book is accurate at the time of going to press, and the publishers and the author cannot accept responsibility for any errors or omissions, however caused. No responsibility for loss or damage occasioned to any person acting, or refraining from action, as a result of the material in this publication can be accepted by the publisher or the author.

Apart from any fair dealing for the purposes of research or private study, or criticism or review, as permitted under the Copyright, Designs and Patents Act 1988, this publication may only be reproduced, stored or transmitted, in any form, or by any means, with the prior permission in writing of the publisher or, in the case of reprographic reproduction, in accordance with the terms of licences issued by the Copyright Licensing Agency. Enquiries concerning reproduction outside those terms should be sent to the publishers at the following address:

IT Governance Publishing
IT Governance Limited
Unit 3, Clive Court
Bartholomew's Walk
Cambridgeshire Business Park
Ely
Cambridgeshire
CB7 4EH
United Kingdom

www.itgovernance.co.uk

© Nathan Clarke 2010
The author has asserted the rights of the author under the Copyright, Designs and Patents Act, 1988, to be identified as the author of this work.

First published in the United Kingdom in 2010
by IT Governance Publishing.

ISBN 978-1-84928-039-6

PREFACE

Computer forensics has become an essential tool in the identification of misuse and abuse of systems. Whilst widely utilised within law enforcement, the rate of adoption by organisations has been somewhat slower, with many organisations focusing upon the traditional security countermeasures to prevent an attack from occurring in the first place. Such an approach is certainly essential, but it is also well understood that no system or network is completely secure. Therefore, organisations will inevitably experience a cyberattack. Moreover, traditional countermeasures do little to combat the significant threat that exists from within the organisation. Computer forensics is an invaluable tool for an organisation in understanding the nature of an incident and being able to recreate the crime.

The purpose of this pocket book is to provide an introduction to the tools, techniques and procedures utilised within computer forensics, and in particular focus upon aspects that relate to organisations. Specifically, the book will look to:

- develop the general knowledge and skills required to understand the nature of computer forensics;
- provide an appreciation of the technical complexities that exist; and
- allow the reader to understand the changing nature of the field and the subsequent effects that it will have upon an organisation.

This will allow managers to better appreciate the purpose, importance and challenges of the domain, and allow technical staff to understand the key processes and procedures that are required.

The final section of the text has been dedicated to resources that will provide the reader with further directions for reading and information on the tools and applications used within the computer forensic domain.

ABOUT THE AUTHOR

Dr Nathan Clarke is a senior lecturer at the Centre for Security, Communications and Network Research at the University of Plymouth and an adjunct lecturer with Edith Cowan University in Western Australia. He has been active in research since 2000, with interests in biometrics, mobile security, intrusion detection, digital forensics and information security awareness. Dr Clarke is also the undergraduate and postgraduate Programme Manager for information security courses at the University of Plymouth.

During his academic career, Dr Clarke has authored over 50 publications in referred international journals and conferences. He is the current co-chair of the Workshop on Digital Forensics & Incident Analysis (WDFIA) and of the Human Aspects of Information Security & Assurance (HAISA) symposium. Dr Clarke has also served on over 40 international conference events and regularly acts as a reviewer for numerous journals, including *Computers & Security*, *IEEE Transactions on Information Forensics and Security*, *The Computer Journal* and *Security and Communication Networks*.

Dr Clarke is a Chartered Engineer, a member of the Institution of Engineering and Technology (IET) and British Computer Society, and is active as a UK representative in International Federation for Information Processing (IFIP) working groups relating to Information Security Management, Information Security Education and Identity Management.

Further information can be found at:

www.plymouth.ac.uk/cscan.

ACKNOWLEDGEMENTS

Thanks are due to Prof Steven Furnell for his insightful feedback on the draft version of the manuscript. Thanks are also due to my partner, Amy, whose invaluable support has helped immensely.

CONTENTS

Chapter 1: The Role of Forensics within Organisations......1
Chapter 2: Be Prepared – Proactive Forensics 7
Chapter 3: Forensic Acquisition of Data 15
Chapter 4: Forensic Analysis of Data 21
Chapter 5: Anti-Forensics and Encryption 31
Chapter 6: Embedded and Network Forensics 35
Conclusion 41
Resources...43
  Specialist books in Computer Forensics 43
  Software and tools 46
  Web resources...50
ITG Resources..55

CHAPTER 1: THE ROLE OF FORENSICS WITHIN ORGANISATIONS

The importance of information security within an organisation is becoming better understood. Regulation, legislation and good governance are all motivators for organisations to consider the role information security plays in protecting data. Whilst better understood, the adoption of good information security practices is far from uniform across all organisations, with enterprise companies faring better than many smaller organisations who are trailing in their knowledge and deployment of secure practices. With the significant growing threat arising from cybercrime and related activities, it is increasingly important that all organisations address the issue of ensuring good information security.

In order to appreciate the need for computer forensics within an organisation, it is important to look at the nature and scale of the threat that exists. Unfortunately, truly understanding the scale of the threat is difficult as the reporting of cybercrime is relatively patchy. Many organisations see such reporting as something that will affect their brand image and reputation. Whilst discussions are being held in some countries about implementing laws to force organisations into reporting incidents, at this stage the industry relies upon survey statistics to appreciate the threat. Many such surveys exist, but four in particular, used together, provide a good oversight of the cybercrime landscape:

- Computer Crime and Security Survey[1] by the Computer Security Institute (CSI) – an annual survey that typically has over 500 respondents with a focus upon the United States and a skew towards Enterprise organisations. This survey is a regularly cited source for understanding the nature of the threat.

---

[1] *CSI Computer Crime and Security Survey*, Richardson R, Computer Security Institute (2008).
www.gocsi.com

1: The Role of Forensics within Organisations

- Global Information Security Survey[2] by Ernst and Young – another annual survey, but with a wider perspective. In 2009, the survey had almost 1900 organisations from over 50 countries across all major industries.
- Information Security Breaches Survey[3] by the UK Department for Business, Enterprise and Regulatory Reform (BERR) – a UK-focused survey with over a 1000 respondents (in 2008). In comparison to the previous two surveys, the nature of the respondent group in this survey is far more focused upon SMEs rather than Enterprise organisations. It is possible, therefore, to appreciate a different perspective on the problem.
- Global Internet Security Threat Report[4] by Symantec – once a twice-yearly publication, the report is now published annually. This report differs from the previous three in that it does not rely upon people to report the findings. Instead, Symantec acquire the information from a variety of sensors and systems deployed throughout the world. The report therefore provides a far more statistically reliable picture on the nature and scale of the threat; however, it fails to illustrate what the consequences are of those threats and what efforts are being made to better secure systems.

Taking a snapshot of the most current surveys at the time of writing, it is clear that the nature and seriousness of the threat is considerable. Looking at the mainstay of cybercrime, malicious software (malware), it can be seen that they still provide a significant threat to systems. The CSI survey in 2008

---

[2] *Outpacing Change: Ernst & Young's 12th Global Information Security Survey*, Ernst & Young (2009).
www.ey.com/publication/vwLUAssets/12th_annual_GISS/$FILE/12th_annual_GISS.pdf

[3] *Information Security Breaches Survey*, BERR (2008), Crown Copyright.
www.berr.gov.uk/files/file45714.pdf

[4] *Symantec Global Internet Security Threat Report: Trends for 2008*, Symantec (2009).
http://eval.symantec.com/mktginfo/enterprise/white_papers/b-whitepaper_internet_security_threat_report_xiv_04-2009.en-us.pdf

1: The Role of Forensics within Organisations

reported that 50% of respondents experienced a virus incident (which includes other forms of malware). The BERR survey reports this as lower at 35% in 2008 overall; however, notably when analysing for Enterprise organisations only, this number shoots back up to 68%. This demonstrates at present, Enterprise organisations are a far larger target for attackers. Indeed, Symantec's report has identified that threats are increasingly being targeted to specific organisations or individuals, and the CSI survey also reported that 27% of respondents had experienced targeted attacks within their organisation.

An underlying theme in this changing threat landscape is the move towards financial reward. Symantec reports that the underground economy is generating millions of dollars in revenue from cybercrime-related activity. Previously, financial reward was infrequently a key driver of cybercrime. Hackers would break into systems in order to demonstrate their technical ability over those administrating the systems, and malware writers created viruses and worms that would maximise their infection and spread throughout the Internet. However, since the beginning of the millennium the surveys have shown an increasing focus being given towards threats that provide a financial reward to the attacker. Advanced-fee fraud and phishing or 419 scams are two examples of widespread threats aimed at providing financial reward. As awareness of these widespread threats increases, so the threat evolves towards more targeted threats, such as spear phishing.

Whilst the previous two trends are focused upon the threats that enter the system from outside the organisation, the surveys point to a considerable threat coming from inside. The CSI survey put this second to virus incidents at 44% of respondents, with the BERR survey at 21%. Moreover, the BERR survey in particular noticed a significant swing from external to internal threat, with over two-thirds of the worst incidents coming from inside misuse. Organisations, therefore, may face a considerable threat from their own employees. This becomes more concerning when you appreciate that much of the traditional information security mechanisms are focused upon

1: The Role of Forensics within Organisations

ensuring that attackers from outside the system cannot get in. Little consideration is frequently given to the attackers from within the system.

Whilst the nature of the threat has changed significantly, it is essential to realise that it is still evolving. Although it is difficult to predict what form the threat will take in the future – largely by doing so will itself ensure the threat evolves in a different direction – it is important to ensure information security is not simply a reactive system that deploys new countermeasures upon identification of new threats, but proactively seeks to develop controls, practices and policies to assist in their identification and prevention.

The discussion up to this point has focused upon cybercrime. However, it is also important to appreciate that information systems are not simply the target of crime but are frequently used as a tool for crime. Many forms of traditional crime, such as money laundering, fraud, blackmail, distribution of child pornography and illegal drug distribution, can all be facilitated by the use of computers. Indeed, given the ubiquitous nature of information systems and the efficiency gains achieved in using them for financial record keeping and communication, it is difficult to envisage many crimes of this nature not using computers. Within an organisational perspective, it is important to ensure you do not simply protect your systems from cybercrime threats, but also ensure they are not being used to facilitate traditional crime.

Digital forensics is a growing specialism that assists organisations in the identification of misuse. In comparison to many areas of traditional information security, such as authentication and access control, it is relatively new, born out of the need to be able to identify exploitation of electronic systems in a manner that would be deemed acceptable by the juridical system. Within digital forensics, a number of more specific sub-categories exist, such as computer, network and embedded forensics. Each in turn seeks to understand their specific technology platform to capitalise upon the evidence being captured. For instance, within computer forensics, tools,

1: The Role of Forensics within Organisations

techniques and procedures have been developed to extract evidence from hard drive and volatile media. Significant time has been focused upon understanding the nature of file systems in order to ensure all artefacts are identified, and to appreciate the nature of the data. Within embedded forensics, such as mobile devices or game consoles, the nature of the underlying architecture means that different tools and procedures are required in order to extract relevant artefacts in a forensically sound manner.

A key driver to date for the use of computer forensics has been from law enforcement and the identification of traditional crime. This quickly moved on to cybercrime, but is still largely within the sphere of law enforcement and their need to analyse systems in a legally acceptable manner in order to bring the guilty to justice. However, although this driver has not changed, organisations are increasingly identifying the importance of establishing a computer forensics expertise. Whilst organisations might not always seek criminal or civil compensation for the attacks against their systems, it has become accepted that the tools, techniques and procedures developed for digital forensics provides an effective and sound methodology for analysing systems. The primary motivation for using forensics is incident management and the ability to identify which files have been affected and how the malware has infected the system, with a view to closing the vulnerability. Forensics within the organisation can also be used to identify possible insider misuse of systems or information. An organisation equipped with a well-trained computer forensic capability is able to both reactively and proactively defend against attacks from both inside and outside the organisation.

The primary focus within the digital forensic industry has been on computer forensics and as such the focus of this pocket book will largely be on computer forensics. However, many of the processes and procedures documented within the forthcoming chapters are also appropriate for use within the other areas. In addition, a chapter has also been included to discuss specific aspects of network and embedded forensics as

1: The Role of Forensics within Organisations

both of these are becoming increasingly important within a world where mobile devices are ubiquitous and anti-forensic techniques are more commonplace. The next three chapters focus upon the core procedural aspects of computer forensics: the proactive stance, acquisition and analysis.

CHAPTER 2: BE PREPARED – PROACTIVE FORENSICS

Within an organisation, undertaking forensics is not a simple task and involves a series of procedural and technical aspects that if not carried out correctly will affect the forensic value of the investigation and the resulting evidence. It is therefore essential that these are developed, implemented and tested prior to tackling an incident. Being proactive about the design of a forensic expertise within your organisation will ensure that your incident response team is able to respond effectively and efficiently. This chapter introduces the steps necessary to be proactive, and discusses the key procedural aspects that need to be followed during an investigation.

Being proactive is not simply about ensuring the correct procedures are in place for dealing with an incident, or about ensuring staff have the necessary training to forensically acquire and analyse machines running Windows®, Linux, Unix and Mac (plus many others). It is possible to go further in the forensic readiness and consider the organisational IT infrastructure. Optimising the IT infrastructure for use within incident analysis will enable more efficient analysis of systems whilst minimising the operational impact on systems. For instance, if an organisation has a file server that is critical to operations and is under a 24/7 service level agreement, then it would be difficult to take a system down for forensic acquisition of data – particularly as this can take some time when dealing with large storage volumes. Establishing redundancy within the IT architecture would assist in ensuring critical systems remain operational yet provide a facility to provide incident analysis.

The most effective deployment of a forensics team is as an aspect of the organisation's Computer Security Incidence Response Team (CSIRT) –more commonly referred to as Computer Emergency Response Team (CERT). Whilst no definitive standard exists to date, Carnegie Mellon University's

2: Be Prepared – Proactive Forensics

CERT have compiled a handbook for the development, implementation and management of a CSIRT.[5] The handbook provides a robust framework for the handling and assessment of incidents, and clearly defines the role for forensics as one belonging to incident analysis.

Whilst it is out of the scope of this text to describe the framework in detail, it is worth highlighting the specific aspects relating to setting up a forensics team. Computer forensics is a highly human-centric process, requiring trained specialists with the specific knowledge of operating systems and forensic software. This therefore places a large burden upon recruitment and training of staff. Furthermore, once trained, given that new operating systems function differently and frequently come equipped with new file systems, resources are required for continued training. The scope of training will depend upon the variety of systems an organisation is using; fewer file systems result in less training. The nature of undertaking forensics means you do not only need an individual with an excellent technical knowledge of systems, but you are also looking for someone who has an inquisitive mind, and is able to identify leads and follow them through the data. Given the complex nature of file systems and the large storage capacities of hard drive media, it simply is not cost effective to examine every aspect of the drive. It is therefore necessary to understand and appreciate the nature of the crime, the resulting evidence that might exist and where such evidence might reside on the media. The results and findings of the forensic investigation are very much down to the examiner and their ability to professionally analyse the data.

The actual process of computer forensics is inherently a reactive approach to the identification of misuse of systems, whether that is cyber or computer-assisted crime. But how do you know when to undertake a forensic investigation of a system? Because of the nature of forensics, specifically the

---

[5] *Handbook for Computer Security Incident Response Teams (CSIRTs)*, West-Brown, M et al, CERT Carnegie Mellon (2003).
www.cert.org/csirts

2: Be Prepared – Proactive Forensics

time and resources required to investigate a system, routine investigation of systems is simply infeasible. An organisation will investigate a system based upon one or more factors causing concern to an administrator. Traditional security controls are frequently used for cyber-related activities, such as Intrusion Detection System (IDS) alarms, a system operating outside of normal parameters, unusual processes running on a system, log files containing spurious entries, network logs showing large volumes of traffic entering or leaving the network, or end-users reporting discrepancies.

Having established that something is amiss, forensics can now be utilised to identify what has happened. Whilst literature differs a little on the number of stages that a forensics procedure requires, all agree on the general principle of the process. Amongst the most robust and popular models proposed is the Digital Forensics Workshop[6] model. It establishes seven key stages to the process:

- Identification – the initial identification that something is wrong and requires forensic investigation.
- Preservation – to ensure data is acquired in a forensically sound manner with an appropriate chain of custody being maintained.
- Collection – the use of approved software and hardware and appropriate legal authority where necessary in collecting the evidence.
- Examination – through the use of filtering and data extraction techniques identify artefacts of interest.
- Analysis – understand the chronology of events and link together artefacts in order to understand the complete picture.
- Presentation – document and present the findings in an appropriate manner.
- Decision – in a legal situation this would be whether sufficient evidence exists to proceed with a criminal case.

---

[6] *DFRWS Technical Report: A Road Map for Digital Forensic Research*, Palmer, G, DFRWS (2001). *www.dfrws.org/2001/dfrws-rm-final.pdf*

2: Be Prepared – Proactive Forensics

Within an organisational environment, it could be the point at which a decision is made to proceed with civil proceedings or an action is taken against an employee.

The core underlying principle within computer forensics is preservation of data. Therefore, during all stages of examination and analysis a forensic examiner will work on duplicates of the original evidence rather than the original. Should changes occur to the data, an additional duplicate of the original can be made. In order to facilitate the preservation of evidence, it is important to ensure an appropriate chain of custody throughout the forensic investigation, from the initial capture of the hardware through to collection, examination, analysis and presentation. At all stages, it should be clear who had been handling the data and when. At no time should the evidence remain unsupervised or freely accessible. In the UK, examiners adhere with the Association of Chief Police Officers (ACPO) guidelines.[7] These comprise of four principles:

1. No action taken by law enforcement agencies or their agents should change data held on a computer or storage media which may be subsequently relied upon in court.

2. In circumstances where a person finds it necessary to access original data held on a computer or on storage media, that person must be competent to do so and be able to give evidence explaining the relevance and the implications of their actions.

3. An audit trial or other record of all processes applied to computer-based electronic evidence should be created and preserved. An independent third party should be able to examine those processes and achieve the same result.

---

[7] *Good Practice Guide for Computer-Based Electronic Evidence*, 7Safe, ACPO (2007).
www.7safe.com/electronic_evidence/ACPO_guidelines_computer_evidence.pdf

2: Be Prepared – Proactive Forensics

4. The person in charge of the investigation (the case officer) has overall responsibility for ensuring that the law and these principles are adhered to.

Whilst the intention of the organisation in performing an investigation might not be one of involving the police or seeking compensation through civil actions, care should always be taken in following these principles in case such a decision is required at a later stage. For instance, in many investigations the true consequences of insider misuse might not be understood until after the investigation has taken place. If the investigation did not follow the guidelines and good forensic practice, the value of the evidence found would be in question.

In addition to the personnel requirements for establishing a forensics expertise, thought must also be given to the equipment required to perform such activities. The subsequent chapters provide an insight into the techniques and tools required to perform a forensic investigation, with the Resources section providing a reference. However, for the moment the dialogue will concentrate on the initial set-up requirements. In order to perform forensic analysis of systems, it is imperative that the machine performing the analysis is a trusted one that has not been compromised. Typically this would involve having a stand-alone computer or, within a larger environment, a closed network with minimal network connections to essential services. A large role of the investigation will be to undertake string searches of the drive for specific keywords or file formats. With large storage devices this takes time, so having sufficient processing capacity and high-speed drives would assist in speeding up the process. A myriad of hardware and software components are then required to perform the actual investigation. Given the nature of the task, it is also important the investigation takes place in a restricted room with strict physical access control. Maintaining the integrity of the investigation is paramount if the organisation decides they wish to utilise the evidence for any formal civil or criminal proceedings.

2: Be Prepared – Proactive Forensics

It is worth highlighting that as computer forensics is a relatively new discipline, the speed of change regarding what is considered standard operating procedure is rapid. New developments within the area are pushing the envelope of what computer forensics is able to achieve. A decade ago, computer forensics involved the use of some elementary tools and hexadecimal editors that allowed you to view the actual data. Tools have since been developed that permit the extraction of files and whole file systems in a forensically sound manner. This has reduced the technical level of expertise required in many cases and has certainly speeded up dramatically the process of examination. The flip side to this is, unfortunately, that examiners now have to deal with far larger storage capacities than they did a decade ago. These advancements are continually being made. For instance, the meaning of the term proactive in forensics is beginning to change from the proactive development of a forensic capability and design of organisation infrastructure to support forensic and incidence analysis to the detection of attacks. This is an extremely useful attribute for an organisation to have as it means forensics is no longer merely a reactive tool to identify what has gone wrong, but can also be used as a mechanism for alerting that something has gone wrong. It is imperative for forensic investigators and organisations to stay on top of these developments as they frequently improve the efficiency and effectiveness of investigations.

Finally, when looking to establish a forensics expertise within your organisation there a variety of factors that must be considered:

- People – cost of setting up the team in terms of recruitment, initial and ongoing training
- Forensic laboratory – development of a forensic laboratory with sufficient equipment to carry out forensic investigations
- Developing appropriate incident response procedures and understanding their effect and impact upon the organisation

2: Be Prepared – Proactive Forensics

- Organisational policy – modifications to the security policy and employee contracts may be required to permit forensic investigation of employee systems
- Organisational IT infrastructure (optional) – development of the IT infrastructure to facilitate forensic investigations.

In order to understand the basics of undertaking a forensic investigation, two key elements need to be discussed. Chapter 3 deals with the first, that of forensic acquisition of hard drive data, and Chapter 4 introduces the techniques used to examine and analyse media.

CHAPTER 3: FORENSIC ACQUISITION OF DATA

A key theme in the digital forensics procedure is one of preservation of data. This is no more important than at the acquisition stage where the investigator has to deal with the original suspect system. Securing data at this stage is imperative for the integrity of the investigation. This chapter focuses upon the procedures and tools available for the acquisition of data on a computer system. It will also give consideration to the decisions an examiner will have to make during the process and the effects they have upon the data integrity.

A computer system fundamentally has two sources of data that are of interest to a forensic examiner: volatile and non-volatile memory. Volatile memory primarily relates to the main RAM of a computer, but also includes cache memory and even register memory. Forensic investigations typically focus upon the main memory, as this has a significantly larger capacity than the other two, with systems commonly having 2–4 gigabytes (GBs) of data. Non-volatile memory relates to all other media types that do not lose their data when the power source is removed. Hard drives are amongst the most common forms of memory, with capacities now in terabytes. However, a variety of removable-based media are now also commonly found (e.g. USB keys/Thumb Drives, iPods and SD cards) with varying storage capacities in the gigabyte range.

The first decision a forensic examiner is faced with is what to do with the suspect machine once an incident has been identified. If the system is switched off, the decision is somewhat simpler as all volatile memory will likely have been lost. If the system remains powered on, the forensic investigator needs to decide whether to power it off immediately, or to perform a live acquisition of the RAM and analysis of the system. Unless the examiner has a suspicion that damage could be done to this or other systems by keeping the machine running, they will typically perform a live

3: Forensic Acquisition of Data

acquisition and analysis. Examples of damage in this situation could include a process running on the machine that is forensically wiping the hard drive, a virus or worm that is corrupting data, or a machine being used to attack another system.

When undertaking a live acquisition and analysis it is imperative that no (or in reality as little as possible) changes are made to the memory. In order to preserve the RAM memory, the first task of the examiner is to forensically copy this data. Once copied, a number of other tools can then be used to extract useful operating information about the system. A wide variety of feely available tools exist that would be used during the live analysis to capture pertinent data. These include:

- arp.exe
- attrib.exe
- cmd.exe
- dd.exe
- drivers.exe
- dumpel.exe
- Fport.exe
- hostname.exe
- ipconfig.exe
- netstat.exe
- net.exe
- netusers.exe
- openports.exe
- ps.exe
- psfile.exe
- psloggedon.exe
- pstat.exe
- routekitrevealer.exe
- route.exe
- sniffer.exe

In order to ensure the integrity of the information received during the live analysis, it is important to ensure you use versions of the tools belonging to you (i.e. trusted) – not those that might inherently be on the system being analysed. As such, it is common for forensic examiners to develop their own suite of tools for use in live acquisition and analysis. The range of tools will depend upon the systems being analysed and the information you wish to capture. Increasingly more commonplace are commercial offerings that provide all the utilities on a single CD or USB drive. For example, e-fense,[8] a

---

[8] Live Response, e-fense (2009).
www.e-fense.com

3: Forensic Acquisition of Data

provider of forensic applications and tools, is one company that provides a self-contained USB key with all the tools and applications required to perform live acquisition and analysis. The Windows Forensic Toolchest™[9] is an alternative open source tool specifically designed for automated incident response and audit.

Once the live analysis is complete, the system can be powered down and taken to the forensic laboratory for acquisition of non-volatile memory. The acquisition of hard drive media (and that of removable media) can be achieved in a number of ways:

- Physically remove the drive from the suspect machine and connect it to the trusted forensic machine. The method of connection to the forensic system will depend upon the type of drive (i.e. IDE, SCSI, SATA) and what the forensic system is able to accept. A wide variety of cables, connectors and converters exist to facilitate this. Having a good mixture of this equipment whilst setting up the forensic laboratory is essential in saving time. When connecting the drive it is standard procedure to use a write blocker in serial between the suspect drive and the forensic machine. The hardware write blocker will not permit any write signals from entering the suspect drive and thus affect the integrity of the data. Again write blockers can be purchased that are able to function with a variety of hard drive types.[10]
- Use a network to establish a connection with the suspect machine. The standard approach here, if the suspect machine is within your physical control, is to boot the machine using a trusted CD or USB memory stick that contains an application to enable network communications and drive acquisition to take place. Your forensics machine then contains the client connection and retrieves the drive

---

[9] Windows Forensic Toolchest, McDougal, M, (2009). www.foolmoon.net/security
[10] Forensic Bridges, Tableau (2010). www.tableau.com

3: Forensic Acquisition of Data

image in a forensically sound manner. EnCase®'s LinEn is a popular example of this.[11]

From an organisational perspective, it is not always possible to follow the previous steps when acquiring hard drive media. Many organisations have mission critical systems that simply must remain on. Therefore, the ideal is not always available. Farmer and Venema[12] suggest four levels of data acquisition, in order of increasing accuracy:

- individual files
- back-up repositories
- individual disk partition – bit-for-bit acquisition
- entire disk – bit-for-bit acquisition.

If the evidence is stored or still remains within existing files, then both the first two approaches would be successful in identifying the artefacts. The advantage of the latter two approaches is the wealth of information that can be obtained from unallocated clusters of memory and the operating system itself. The latter two are also distinguishable from the former by the bit-for-bit acquisition process. To forensically acquire a drive, the ideal is to acquire every bit of information from the drive, so that a complete picture can be formed of the data that is stored. Thinking realistically this is logical as people will always tend to hide their criminal activities, and often by the time the forensic investigation has begun, much of the evidence may no longer reside on the active file system.

A variety of bit-for-bit tools exists to facilitate the duplication process. The main decision to consider is whether you want a raw duplicate copy or a compressed image. The original method of forensically copying drives was by creating a raw duplicate image of the drive. The Unix command 'dd' was widely adopted for this as it performed a bit-for-bit copy. This would mean, in order to copy a 250GB drive, the examiner

---

[11] EnCase® eDiscovery, Guidance Software (2010). www.guidancesoftware.com
[12] *Forensic Discovery*, Farmer, D, and Venema, W, Addison Wesley (2005), ISBN: 0321525507.

3: Forensic Acquisition of Data

would also need a 250GB or larger drive to store the duplicate image. It is also important when reusing drives in the forensic laboratory that drives are either new or forensically wiped to ensure data from the previous investigation does not leak through to the new investigation. The newer method of imaging is to compress the image. Applications designed to do this tend to be proprietary, but have the advantage of being able to add additional metadata to the image and compress the overall size of the image, making storage of image data far more efficient. Guidance Software, AccessData and New Technologies, Inc. (NTI) all provide data acquisition tools that create compressed images (see *Resources* section for more information).

The chapter began by referring to the fact that preservation of data is imperative at this stage. The process of ensuring preservation of data comes from traditional information security and the need to ensure integrity of data. The universal tool used for this is the Hash Function. A Hash Function is able to take a variable length input and produce a fixed length output that will uniquely identify the input, often referred to as a fingerprint of the data. Two algorithms have traditionally been utilised:

- Message Digest 5 (MD5) – a 128-bit output created by Ronald Rivest[13]
- Secure Hashing Algorithm (SHA-1) – a 160-bit output published by NIST[14]

By hashing and acquiring a fingerprint of the suspect drive before acquisition and then comparing that output with the hashed output of the duplicate drive, an examiner is able to verify that an exact bit-for-bit copy of the drive has been produced. Hashing can also be applied to files, folders or partitions to ensure that upon acquisition and subsequent analysis the examiner has not modified the data in any way.

---

[13] *The MD5 Message-Digest Algorithm*, Rivest, R, Network Working Group RFC1321 (1992). www.ietf.org/rfc/rfc1321.txt

[14] *FIBS PUB 180-1: Secure Hash Standard*, NIST (1995). www.itl.nist.gov/fipspubs/fip180-1.htm

3: Forensic Acquisition of Data

Once the drive or partition has been acquired and the integrity verified, the examiner need no longer work with the original suspect drive or system. Indeed, it is standard procedure to carefully store the original evidence under lock and key in order to maintain the chain of custody, giving careful consideration to environmental factors that might impact upon the quality of the evidence (e.g. placing hard drives near magnetic sources). Creating a second duplicate of the drive is also common practice to help ensure the original drive is never required again. If changes are made to the duplicate drive, the second drive can be used to reimage the drive.

Acquisition and storage of hard drive media is an essential step in the computer forensics procedure. Whilst tools are freely available to undertake this process, careful consideration is required over the hardware, software and procedures an organisation is to take; incompatibilities between hard drive interfaces, access to the BIOS for modifying the boot sequence, driver versions, organisational policies and logistics can all hinder the acquisition. However, once successfully acquired, the drive can then be analysed.

CHAPTER 4: FORENSIC ANALYSIS OF DATA

The purpose of this chapter is to provide an insight into how to undertake an analysis of a forensic image. General topics will be discussed, such as dead analysis and file carving. However, the nature of an analysis is very much dependent upon the underlying file system being used by the operating system. Owing to its popularity, this chapter will specifically focus upon the Windows® file and operating system. How to identify forensic evidence from various aspects of the system, such as file slack, e-mail, Internet history and virtual memory, will all be discussed.

The process of forensically analysing images very much depends upon the suspected nature of the incident. For instance, malware incidents will leave very different artefacts to cases where employees have been misusing computer systems (e.g. downloading and/or distributing pornography). For those incidents involving people, it is also important to consider the technical capability of the individual involved. Those with more technical knowledge potentially have the ability to hide data within the system more effectively, therefore requiring a different approach and level of analysis.

The analysis of the drive can be achieved in two ways: live and dead analysis. Traditionally, the forensic procedure has focused upon dead analysis – analysing the forensic image from your trusted forensic system. The data on the image never changes and the integrity of the data is therefore simpler to maintain. For most investigations, this form of analysis is sufficient. A live analysis is where you would utilise the operating system (OS) on the suspect image to collect evidence – booting from the suspect image. Within dead analysis, forensic file system analysers are able to interpret a specific file system, and subsequently recreate the file system for you. In order to achieve this the analysers must understand the exact nature of the file system – from the location and operation of the file system, to interpreting the file record metadata. Prior to these

4: Forensic Analysis of Data

tools being available, the forensic examiner would have difficulty in establishing file pathways and understanding the structure of the file system, without performing a live analysis – where the host OS would interpret the file system for the examiner. File system analysers also allow the examiner to acquire all the metadata about the files and folders, such as modified, accessed and created timestamps, which is essential in understanding an investigation. Numerous such analysers now exist: EnCase®, FTK® and Autopsy are three popular tools (see *Resources* section for more information). Figure 1 below provides an illustration of the output that can be seen from such a tool. The tool has a number of key areas: the file system tree view (on the upper left in Figure 1); a folder list (on the upper right in Figure 1); and a detailed file view (lower right in Figure 1).

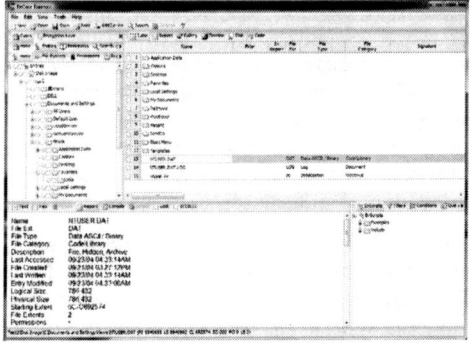

Figure 1: Screenshot of the file system from EnCase®

In addition to recreating the file system, these tools will also identify and list deleted folders and files that are still present within the file system. The extent to which the file is actually still present depends upon the state of the system at any particular point in time. Various situations arise with regards to deleted files:

4: Forensic Analysis of Data

- The file system still contains the record with all metadata and file data.
- The file system contains the record with metadata, but the file contents themselves have been overwritten.
- The file system no longer contains the record with metadata, but the file contents still exist on the image.

In addition to these situations, the nature of the file contents can also be partially overwritten. The ability for a forensic examiner to retrieve the information in a partially overwritten case depends upon which bytes of the file are overwritten and which tools are being used. In the first two cases, the analyser will list what information is available within the file system view and, where possible, link to the file itself. In the final situation, the file system is unable to list the file, but performing file carving and string searches on the complete drive can reveal these.

Before proceeding to explain forensic analysis further, it is necessary to briefly introduce file systems. Each file system operates differently and is technically complicated, but their operation can be highly valuable to a forensic examiner; they will frequently perform tasks that a user is unaware of and that could contain artefacts of interest. For instance, when deleting a file in Windows®, a user may consider the file to be removed from the drive, whereas the file system simply marks the entry in the file system as available. In order to be able to undertake a forensic analysis of a system it is therefore imperative that the examiner has the knowledge and understanding of the system in order to ensure they know where to look for evidence. A number of specific texts have been written on the different file systems to assist the forensic examiner – information on these are located in the *Resources* section.

The discussion from this point will cover the New Technology File System (NTFS) and the Windows® OS. However, many of the techniques and procedures are also valid for other systems. The discussion will focus upon the primary methods used to analyse a system:

- common techniques for investigation

4: Forensic Analysis of Data

- exploring user activity and communication
- file carving
- virtual memory
- registry.

If you are performing an investigation where the source of evidence is not a bit-for-bit copy (i.e. a back-up dataset) the only approaches available to the examiner are the first and second methods. The remaining approaches assume a bit-for-bit copy of the hard drive with the final two methods only available if the drive image has an OS installed on it.

Common investigative techniques include simple searches through the file system for file and data of interest to the investigation. The 'My Documents' folder for an individual could be valuable source of evidence if the person concerned has been saving information pertaining to the incident. Looking through the Recycle Bin and within the deleted folders and files would also be a useful place to start. A primary tool for the investigator is being able to search through the drive for keywords or file types. If you are looking for images, you can perform a search to find all jpeg or bitmap images, etc. A very simply hiding technique used by novice computer users is to modify the file extension to something else in order to avoid such searches. However, most commercially available tools such as EnCase® and FTK®, are able to verify the signature of the files to ensure the file extension matches the file header. These keyword searches are able to scan through the entire disk, including unallocated clusters.

In order to reduce the number of files requiring analysis, it is useful to remove all files that pertain to the OS and standard applications. Hash values of every file can be compared to a reference source. Those with matching hash values are trusted files and can therefore be removed from the analysis. NIST has developed the National Software Reference Library (NSRL),[15] which is freely available and integrates into many forensic

---

[15] National Software Reference Library, NIST (2010).
www.nsrl.nist.gov

4: Forensic Analysis of Data

analysers. This significantly reduces the burden upon the investigator. It is also extremely useful in malware and hacking investigations as it quickly becomes evident which OS files have been infected or modified.

Once the basic level of analysis has been completed and all the obvious places of interest have been investigated, the examiner can turn to analysing application-specific data. As applications tend to create temporary information during their operation, these can be used to identify what has been happening. Which applications the examiner will investigate will depend upon the nature of the investigation; if the incident is concerned with illegal access to a database system, the focus for the investigator will be upon the database application logs. Common applications that are investigated, however, include web browsers, e-mail and instant messenger clients, and office documents. In each of these cases, the files (temporary or not) created by the application tend to be proprietary and are therefore stored in a proprietary format. The choices for the examiner in this situation are:

- Obtain information from the Software Vendor on the structure and format of the file. View the file in hexadecimal and translate the contents.
- Install the application on a forensics machine. Extract the file of interest and use the application to view the file contents.
- Use an inbuilt viewer within the forensics tool to view the file.

For common applications such as web browsers, e-mail clients and image viewers, commercial forensic tools contain an inbuilt viewer to view the proprietary files. For example, Figure 2 below illustrates the view from EnCase® when analysing e-mail. For other applications, the examiner will need to extract the file and use the application to view the file. It is extremely time intensive to go to the effort of understanding and translating the file structure. However, with many organisations having bespoke applications this is sometimes necessary.

4: Forensic Analysis of Data

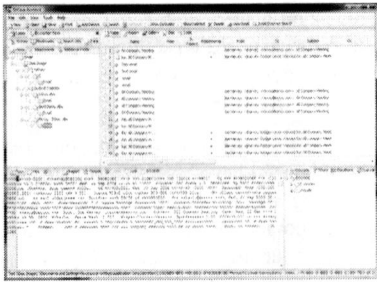

Figure 2: An illustration of EnCase®'s e-mail history view

Before discussing file carving, it is worthwhile to introduce the concept of file slack. File slack is one reason why bit-for-bit duplication of drives is useful to the examiner. File slack is an area of memory on the drive that can contain valuable information from deleted files. In order to understand file slack, some hard drive and operating system details are required. The smallest area of memory on a hard drive is referred to as a sector. In Windows®, a sector is typically 512 bytes. Sectors are then grouped into clusters, with a cluster having 1–128 sectors. From a file system perspective, the smallest data area that is indexed are clusters. As illustrated in Figure 3, when the OS is writing to a disk, should the file it is writing not be an exact multiple of the cluster size, then an area of memory will be left remaining. This is referred to as file slack. Every complete unused sector within the cluster simply does not change. Therefore, any contents previously stored on those sectors will remain. In addition, the hard drive itself must write in sector chunks. Should the file contents stop midway through a sector, the OS will fill the remaining sector with data. In older versions of Windows® (such as Windows® 98) the contents for this used to come from the RAM, which potentially is an extremely useful source of evidence; however, newer versions of the OS simply zero out that space. This type of slack is commonly referred to as RAM slack.

4: Forensic Analysis of Data

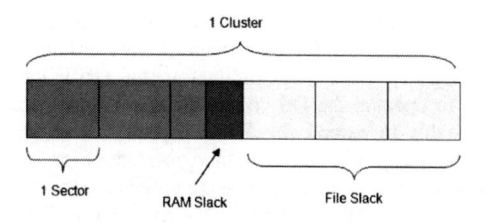

Figure 3: RAM and file slack

The problem with file slack is that it simply contains file data. In many cases, all of the metadata associated to the file and stored in the file system (the Master File Table (MFT) in NTFS) is lost. Therefore, the examiner would not know the file existed. This is where a process called file carving comes in very useful. File carvers do not need any metadata knowledge of the file but simply trawl through the disk looking for file headers and footers. Once the start and end of a file have been identified, the file can be extracted or carved from the disk. In addition to file slack, file carving is also extremely useful when searching through unallocated areas of memory.[16]

Given the dynamic nature of the file system, many files in slack space and unallocated memory no longer have the complete file contents still intact. Frequently, only partial file fragments exist with bits of the header, footer or file contents missing. Moreover, many files are stored on disk in non-sequential order (i.e. fragmented), making it difficult for a file carver to simply extract all data from the beginning of the header to the end of the footer. Therefore, a variety of file carving mechanisms have been develop to assist in extracting the files such as semantic carving, fragment recovery carving and SmartCarving (see *Resources* section for further information).

---

[16] Unallocated areas of memory are clusters that the file system is not currently using. However, this is not to say these clusters were not previously used and therefore will still contain the file contents of what was previously stored there.

4: Forensic Analysis of Data

Within a Windows® OS, there are two further aspects of particular interest to a forensic examiner: the virtual memory and the Registry. When a system does not have sufficient RAM memory to operate, the OS creates a space on the hard drive and uses this to extend the RAM capacity. Referred to as virtual memory, this file can be considerable in size and contain RAM-based memory from the previous session. During each new session, the memory is overwritten with the new session data – although file slack data of previous sessions can still remain. This is one reason why care should be taken when booting from the suspect drive, as previous session information will be overwritten and lost. The size of this file can be in the order of gigabytes. Whilst the discussion has focused upon hard drive analysis, RAM-based data can also be extremely useful in understanding what the user and/or system was doing during the last session. This area of memory can also contain a variety of artefacts such as encryption keys and passwords. The virtual memory, therefore, is a useful source to examine further. On Windows® XP systems, this file is named 'pagefile.sys' and can be located under the root directory of the drive. Analysing this type of file, however, is more difficult than others because of the lack of file structure. With other files, a header, footer and file structure exists for understanding the file. With the virtual memory, this understanding remains with the active OS and therefore the file contains no structure. As a result, the examiner needs to perform a series of string searches on the file in order to try and identify relevant artefacts.

The remaining area of discussion for this chapter is the Registry. The Registry is a hierarchical database that contains the configuration settings for the OS and applications. It is the Registry that also contains the user's authentication credentials. As a vast source of information about the system, what has been installed, when the system was last running, who the users are, what network cards are present, etc, the Registry is an extremely useful source of evidence. The Registry is not stored on the file system as a single file, but is stored principally in

4: Forensic Analysis of Data

five files: Sam, Security, Software, System, Default.[17] The OS is responsible for creating the Registry when loading. Obviously, when forensically analysing the system, unless you are performing a live analysis, the Registry will not exist as a whole but as separate files. In this situation, like the procedure for proprietary files, you can extract the files and then use a Registry viewer to understand the contents, or use some commercial software like EnCase® or FTK® and use the built-in Registry viewer to extract the information for you.

The chapter has provided a preliminary insight into the forensic analysis of media, demonstrating that evidence can be located in a variety of areas. Even data thought to be lost for some time, might still reside on the drive in unallocated memory or file slack. Unfortunately, owing to the dynamic nature of the file system, it is difficult to predict exactly what will or will not be present at any point in time. It is therefore imperative that systems are acquired speedily upon identification of an incident. For links to further information on forensic analysis of computers please refer to the Resources section.

---

[17] 'Windows Registry Information for Advanced Users', Microsoft (2008). *http://support.microsoft.com/kb/256986*

CHAPTER 5: ANTI-FORENSICS AND ENCRYPTION

As computer forensics becomes better understood, a variety of tools and techniques have been developed to hide evidence, remove artefacts or restrict forensic analysis. Tools, for instance, include the ability to forensically delete Internet histories so that organisations are not able to establish misuse, and the ability to modify timestamps so that establishing a chronology of an incident is impossible. This chapter will introduce the topic of anti-forensics and encryption, and explain to what extent it can hinder a forensic investigation.

The use of cryptography to secure the data is increasing and introduces a significant barrier for the forensic examiner. The nature of the encryption can vary from complete hard drive encryption through either hardware or software means or encryption of particular folders and files. Indeed, it is not uncommon to use both approaches, as the key used to encrypt the drive is universal to all contents on the drive, and there might be files that a user wishes to protect further. The forensic examiner must consider each and decide upon an appropriate procedure.

In some cases it is possible to retrieve the key material through legal means, with legislation such as the UK Regulation of Investigatory Powers Act (RIPA),[18] but this is only open to law enforcement agencies to enforce.[19] Therefore, from an organisational perspective, the examiner will need to look to other approaches. Cracking the cryptography is certainly not a viable approach. Modern cryptography is far too effective for brute force attacks. Establishing whether known weaknesses or vulnerabilities exist against the specific technology or

---

[18] Regulation of Investigatory Powers Act, Crown Copyright (2000). *www.opsi.gov.uk/acts/acts2000/ukpga_20000023_en_1*

[19] It is an interesting aside from an organisational perspective, however, to highlight the need for an organisation to manage and store their key material. Failure to provide the key material when requested will result in a breach of the act.

5: Anti-Forensics and Encryption

application and being able to break the protocol is a possibility. But again, examiners would only ever use known weaknesses rather than looking to find one. The most effective method is to locate the key material and crack the password that protects it if required. A variety of password crackers exist with varying functionality from recovering Windows® log-in passwords and revealing cached passwords to recovering passwords from sniffing the network. Table 1 below illustrates a few of the more notable examples.

Tool Name	Description
Cain & Abel	Recovers a variety of passwords from Windows® systems
L0phtCrack	Windows® password recovery
Ophcrack	Cracks Windows® passwords using Rainbow tables. Interestingly, this tool is also able to crack the more secure NTLM hashes as well as the LM.

Table 1: Password cracking software

From a forensics perspective, one of the most valuable opportunities for capturing this data is during a live analysis. After all, if the system is up and running, the hard drive is being decrypted, and if applications are in operation that require passwords, the key material required in achieving this could well be contained within the RAM. However, this is not necessarily a simple task, as the examiner has to trawl through gigabytes of unstructured data in search of the key.

In addition to being a legitimate tool advocated by information security practitioners, encryption is also a tool that assists an attacker in obfuscating the data, and thereby making the tool a

5: Anti-Forensics and Encryption

of probabilities as the extracted data will simply appear to be random. With the presence of user-friendly steganography tools such as S-Tools,[22] the ability for the technically naïve to utilise steganography is very simple, yet the ability for examiners to identify sources of steganography is increasingly challenging.

In addition, there are a variety of tools whose purpose is completely illicit. The Metasploit Anti-Forensics Project,[23] for instance, have developed a number of tools that would directly affect the value of information obtained during an investigation:

- Timestomp – can modify all four NTFS timestamp values
- Slacker – allows you to hide files within the file slack of the NTFS system
- SAM Juicer – dumps the hashes from the SAM and does so without leaving any trace on the hard drive.

The existence of such tools is beginning to raise some questions over the reliability of evidence gleamed from forensic investigations, with some suggesting that such evidence has little legal grounding.[24] It is certainly evident with such tools that caution should be placed on the evidence obtained from simply the forensic investigation of a single system. Rather a wider variety of sources are required, both forensic and traditional, to ensure that a more appropriate perspective of the incident is obtained.

---

[22] S-Tools (2010). Available from *www.jjtc.com/Security/stegtools.htm*
[23] 'Metasploit Anti-Forensics Project', Liu, V, (2010). *www.metasploit.com/research/projects/antiforensics*
[24] 'The Rise of Anti-Forensics', Berinato, S, CXO Media (2007). *www.csoonline.com/article/221208/The_Rise_of_Anti_Forensics*

5: Anti-Forensics and Encryption

valuable asset for any hacker. Indeed, a number of tools reside in the grey space between legitimate and illegitimate. Packers, virtualisation and steganography all have legitimate purposes, but are also frequently used by hackers to evade detection. It is outside the scope of this text to discuss every aspect; however, steganography in particular is a topic being given an increasing focus.

Steganography is the science of hiding data where nobody (apart from the sender and intended recipient, if applicable) suspects the existence of the message. With cryptography, whilst information is unreadable without the key material to decrypt the message, the examiner is still aware of the existence of the message – which in itself will raise sufficient suspicion to want to decode the message. With steganography, the data to be kept secure is hidden within another, typically benign, file. Whilst the examiner is aware of the benign file, they have no awareness of the hidden data – effectively acting as a covert channel. The data or file to be hidden is placed within a carrier file. Whilst carrier files could be anything, images, music and video files are frequently used. There are also a variety of mechanisms used to achieve steganography – the earliest types simply modified the least significant bits of information that determine the meaningful content of the original file. With images, this would result in an image that is indistinguishable from the original using the naked eye.

Whilst tools such as StegAlyzerSS[20] and StegSecret[21] attempt to detect the presence of steganography, given the variety of mechanisms for how this can be achieved, the reliability of such tools is questionable. They can only test and detect for steganography using mechanisms and approaches that are known about. If you subsequently apply cryptography to the hidden message prior to applying steganography, the challenge of identifying whether the image has hidden data becomes one

---

[20] StegAlyzerSS – Steganography Analyser Signature Scanner, SARC (2010). *http://sarc-wv.com/products/stegalyzerss.aspx*

[21] 'StegSecret: A Simple Steganalysis Tool ;)', Munoz, A, (2007). *http://stegsecret.sourceforge.net*

CHAPTER 6: EMBEDDED AND NETWORK FORENSICS

The aim of this chapter is to provide an insight into the establishing discipline of embedded and network forensics. With embedded devices now encompassing a variety of everyday systems such as mobile phones, personal video recorders (PVRs) and game consoles, the ability to analyse those systems for forensic evidence can be key to establishing what happened in an incident. Furthermore, whilst computer and embedded forensics are able to establish evidence and events within systems, the increasing connectivity of devices means large volumes of evidence may reside on a variety of network appliances. Network forensics is useful for evidence gathering as it often provides a valuable overview of communications, and frequently is not within the control of the perpetrator and therefore subject to abuse.

Whilst computer forensics has formed the mainstay of digital forensics, the ubiquitous nature of mobile devices[25] has made them increasingly interesting targets for investigation. Indeed with over 3 billion mobile subscribers worldwide, penetration of mobile devices is higher than PCs. Moreover, the last decade has seen the mobile device transition from a simple telephony device, with minimal forensic evidence other than calling behaviour, to full-functioning mobile computers with the ability to access a variety of data-orientated services. As such, the potential value of evidence on mobile devices has also increased substantially.

Analysing the anatomy of a mobile device, it can be seen that forensic evidence typically resides on one of three areas: the Subscriber Identity Module (SIM); on-board memory; and an external storage card. The primary purpose of the SIM is to

---

[25] Whilst the term mobile device refers to mobile phones, Smartphones, Personal Digital Assistants (PDAs), netbooks, notebooks and laptops, the primary focus of the discussion is with respect to mobile phone/Smartphone devices.

6: Embedded and Network Forensics

enable authentication of the device to the mobile network. However, it also has a limited space of memory to store contact details, calls made and received, and details of text messages. The SIM also stores a variety of network- and device-based information, but this tends to be of more interest to law enforcement investigations where they also have the ability to analyse the mobile operator's network. From an organisational perspective, an examiner would be more interested in establishing whether the device is being misused. Call and text records could certainly provide some evidence. The newer USIM (for use on the 3G networks) does have the capacity to store more information than the standard SIM. The other areas of memory, the on-board and external storage cards, have the opportunity to deliver more as their storage capacities are far larger. The simpler of the two memories to analyse are the external storage cards (e.g. SD memory). These can be analysed using the same software and techniques discussed for hard drives. Whilst not containing an operating system, the media does have a standard file system and file system analysers are compatible. On-board memory is a little more challenging for the examiner largely because of the myriad of device technologies that exist in the market place. These devices all typically connect to computers with a variety of non-standardised connections, if they connect at all, with the phones themselves running a number of different operating systems. The forensic examiner therefore needs to come equipped with the necessary hardware and software to be able to forensically image and analyse the data. Until more recently, the tools and techniques available were few and far between, frequently requiring bespoke implementations to extract the image from specific models of device. The situation has now improved with a number of commercial vendors providing solutions to forensically analyse a wide variety of the common models – the Oxygen Forensic Suite[26] and Paraben's Device

---

[26] Oxygen Forensic Suite, Oxygen Software (2010). *www.oxygen-forensic.com/en*

6: Embedded and Network Forensics

Seizure[27] are two such products. On-board memory also tends to be largely volatile in nature, so procedures are necessary to ensure the device remains sufficiently powered in order to retain the contents.

Mobile devices represent one form of embedded device. However, as technology penetrates every aspect of life, so a large variety of other embedded devices have come along. The degree to which they will have a use within an investigation will largely depend upon the nature of the investigation, with some devices storing very little data and others storing much more. The general rule of thumb is if the device is able to store information, it potentially has some value to an investigation. Game consoles, such as the Sony PlayStation® and Microsoft®'s Xbox can both contain 250GB hard drives, are network connected and have Internet browsers capable of accessing e-mail, instant messenger and the Internet. Users effectively have the ability to use the console as a normal computer – therefore potentially having the same evidentiary value as normal PCs. Other embedded devices could include PVRs, satellite navigation and MP3 players to name a few of the more common devices. Forensically acquiring and analysing these devices is currently still confined to specialist companies and research laboratories. Whilst it will not be long before such tools and procedures do exist, the only problem is keeping up with the speed of change in technology – new mobile and embedded devices are being developed regularly. This poses a significant challenge to forensic examiners.

The final area of discussion focuses upon network forensics. This area of analysis has become useful for a variety of reasons:

- To provide a means for establishing an incident has taken place and requires investigation.
- To analyse network traffic and understand the nature of a cybercrime attack.

---

[27] Paraben Device Seizure v3.3, Paraben (2010).
www.paraben-forensics.com/catalog/product_info.php?products_id=4 05

6: Embedded and Network Forensics

- To analyse network traffic from a suspect computer when the computer is not available for computer forensics.
- To analyse network traffic records when the data retrieved from computer forensics cannot be trusted.
- To provide a fuller picture for the forensic investigation.

The first of these reasons is by far the most significant for network forensics. Indeed, the terms network forensics and incident analysis frequently are used interchangeably to describe the same process – that of reconstructive traffic analysis. From an incident readiness perspective, your organisation needs to establish appropriate network monitors within the IT infrastructure to capture all network-based traffic. The purpose of these monitors is simply to capture all data within the network for subsequent analysis should it be deemed necessary; for instance, should an IDS alarm, examiners then have the network traffic data to search through to identify the problem. This requires some thought in terms of the volumes of data being captured, the ability of the network capture not to drop packets, and the storage and management of the data.

In terms of practical tools, network forensics to date utilise fundamental tools for the capture and analysis of data, many open source. A network sniffer such as tcpdump[28] can be used for the traffic capture, and tools such as Wireshark[29] can be used to analyse traffic and provide protocol analysis. NetworkMiner[30] is also an open source NFAT for Windows® that interestingly provides a host-centric perspective of the network traffic.

Embedded devices and network forensics are also useful as additional sources to verify or corroborate evidence found on a system. With network forensics, the system is typically not under the control of the suspect, so a greater degree of trust can

---

[28] tcpdump (2009).
www.tcpdump.org
[29] Wireshark Foundation (2010).
www.wireshark.org
[30] NetworkMiner (2010). *http://networkminer.sourceforge.net*

6: Embedded and Network Forensics

be attributed to the findings. With embedded devices, the volume of such devices and their differing technical constructions make removal of all evidence difficult. With the increasing growth of anti-forensic techniques, verifying and corroborating evidence will become increasingly important as single sources of evidence become less reliable.

CONCLUSION

The forensic examination of electronic systems has undoubtedly been a huge success in the identification of cyber and computer-assisted crime. Organisations are placing an increasing importance on the need to be equipped with appropriate incident management capabilities to handle misuse of systems. Computer forensics is an invaluable tool in the process.

The domain of computer forensics has grown considerably in the last decade. Driven by industry, focus was initially placed upon developing tools and techniques to assist in the practical application of the technology. In more recent years, an increasing volume of academic research is being produced exploring various new approaches to obtaining forensic evidence. Each year, these new advances provide significant practical enhancements to forensic examiners.

Whilst these advances are being made, so too are advancements in technology, with larger hard drive media, Storage Area Networks (SANs), increasing variety of mobile and embedded devices, ubiquitous networking across different stakeholder networks (corporate, fixed line ISP, mobile ISP, cellular mobile network) and the interaction of all these technologies within a single incident. As the majority of incidents benefit from forensic analysis, the burden placed upon the forensic examiner to ensure an appropriate level of analysis and examination has taken place is increasing significantly.

Appreciating the change of technology, and understanding the nature of the threat, the evolving discipline of anti-forensics and increasing application of cryptography, the domain of forensics has an extremely challenging and exciting future ahead of it. However, the need for organisations to equip themselves with a forensic capability is becoming essential in order to combat and manage incidents effectively.

RESOURCES

The computer forensics industry is well supported with software and reading material, much of which is freely available online. The purpose of this section is to provide a reference guide for computer forensic materials. The reference is split into the following sections:

- specialist computer forensic books
- software and tools for undertaking all stages of the forensic process
- useful online resources.

Specialist books in Computer Forensics

General books

Building a Digital Forensic Laboratory: Establishing and Managing a Successful Facility
Jones, A, Valli, C
Publisher: Butterworth-Heinemann
ISBN: 978-18561-710-4

Computer Forensics
Newman, C
Publisher: Taylor and Francis Ltd
ISBN: 978-08493-561-0

Computer Forensics: Incident Response Essentials
Kruse, W, Heiser, J
Publisher: Addison Wesley
ISBN: 978-020170-719-9

Digital Evidence and Computer Crime
Casey, E
Publisher: Academic Press
ISBN: 978-012163-104-8

Resources

Digital Forensics for Network, Internet and Cloud Computing: A Forensic Evidence Guide for Moving Targets and Data
Garrison, C
Publisher: Syngress
ISBN: 978-159749-537-0

EnCase Computer Forensics: The Official EnCE – EnCase Certified Examiner Study Guide
Bunting, S
Publisher: John Wiley and Sons
ISBN: 978-047018-145-1

Forensic Computing: A Practitioner's Guide
Sammes, J, Jenkinson, B
Publisher: Springer
ISBN: 978-18462-837-0

Handbook of Digital Forensics and Investigation
Casey, E
Publisher: Academic Press
ISBN: 978-012374-267-4

Incident Response and Computer Forensics
Mandia, K, Prosise, C
Publisher: McGraw-Hill Osborne
ISBN: 978-007222-692-2

Incident Response: Computer Forensics Toolkit
Schweitzer, D
Publisher: John Wiley and Sons
ISBN: 978-076452-636-7

Malware Forensics: Investigating and Analyzing Malicious Code
Malin, C, Casey, E, Aquilina, J
Publisher: Syngress
ISBN: 978-159749-268-3

Real Digital Forensics: Computer Security and Incident Response
Jones, K, Bejtlich, R, Rose, C

Resources

Publisher: Addison Wesley
ISBN: 978-032124-069-9

File and operating system specific books

File System Forensic Analysis
Carrier, B
Publisher: Addison Wesley
ISBN: 978-032126-817-4

Macintosh OS X, iPod and iPhone Forensic Analysis DVD Toolkit
Varsalone, J
Publisher: Syngress
ISBN: 978-159749-297-3

UNIX Forensic Analysis DVD Toolkit
Pogue, C, Altheide, C, Haverkos, T
Publisher: Syngress
ISBN: 978-159749-269-0

Virtualization and Forensics: A Digital Forensic Investigator's Guide to Virtual Environments
Barrett, D, Kipper, G
Publisher: Syngress
ISBN: 978-159749-557-8

Windows Forensic Analysis with DVD Toolkit
Carvey, H
Publisher: Syngress
ISBN:978-159749-422-9

Windows Forensics: The Field Guide for Corporate Computer Investigations
Steel, C
Publisher: John Wiley and Sons
ISBN: 978-047003-862-8

Resources

Network forensic books

Mastering Windows Network Forensics and Investigation
Anson, S, Bunting, S
Publisher: John Wiley and Sons
ISBN: 978-047009-762-5

Computer Forensics: Investigating Network Intrusions and Cyber Crime
EC-Council
Publisher: Course Technology
ISBN: 978-143548-352-9

CISCO Router and Switch Forensics: Investigating and Analyzing Malicious Activity
Liu, D (Editor)
Publisher: Syngress
ISBN: 978-159749-418-2

Network Forensics: Tapping the Internet
Garfinkel, S
Publisher: O'Reilly Media

Mobile device forensics

iPhone Forensics: Recovering Evidence, Personal Data and Corporate Assets
Zdziarski, J
Publisher: O'Reilly Media
ISBN: 978-059615-358-8

Software and tools

The tools listed in the following pages are primarily related to the acquisition and analysis of a Windows®-based system from a Windows®-based forensic station. However, a number of the tools also provide wider OS compatibility, with all of the case management tools for instance supporting the majority of common file systems. There are of course also a wide variety of other forensic tools that operate on Unix and Mac OS X platforms – links to general websites for more information can be found in the Web resources section.

Case management tools

Case management tools are software applications or distributions capable of handling the complete forensic investigation from acquisition through to examination, analysis and presentation.

Guidance Software

Guidance software produces several forensic-related products. Their primary product, EnCase®, is amongst the market leaders in providing forensic investigation of media.

Other products available from Guidance Software include:

- EnCase Enterprise
- EnCase eDiscovery
- EnCase Portable

Web: *www.guidancesoftware.com*

AccessData

AccessData produces several products within the digital forensic domain. A market leader, its primary product the Forensic Toolkit® provides full case management of investigations.

Other products available from AccessData include:

- FTK® Mobile Phone Examiner
- AccessData® Enterprise
- AccessData® eDiscovery
- AccessData® Classified Spillage Solution
- password cracking tools

Web: *www.accessdata.com*

Resources

e-fense

e-fense produces a series of products. The principal product HELIX has its foundations in the open source domain, with a self-bootable CD that contains a suite of tools for undertaking a variety of forensic investigation activities. The majority of the tools available on the CD were produced by other developers and are made freely available. HELIX 3 PRO is now available to purchase from e-fense.

Other products by e-fense also include:

- HELIX 3 Enterprise
- Live Response

Web: *www.e-fense.com*

Technology Pathways

Technology Pathways also provide case management software in the form of their ProDiscover® Forensics software. Their other product, ProDiscover® Incident Response, provides over the network preview and acquisition of data.

Web: *www.techpathways.com*

The Sleuth Kit

An open source suite of tools for forensic investigation. The kit is not a simple application as with many of the previous commercial tools, but does provide a comprehensive toolkit for the analysis of hard drive media. To support the usability, the kit also includes Autopsy, an HTML front-end tool.

Web: *www.sleuthkit.org*

Data acquisition tools

The tools listed below are in addition to the case management tools listed above which are all able to acquire images from hard drives.

Resources

AccessData FTK Imager
Web: www.accessdata.com

EnCase LinEn
Web: www.encase.com

New Technologies SafeBack
Web: www.forensics-intl.com

Paraben Data Arrest
Web: www.paraben-forensics.com

File carving tools

Adriot Photo Forensics
Web: http://digital-assembly.com

DataLifter – File Extractor
Web: www.datalifter.com/products.htm

Foremost
Web: http://foremost.sourceforge.net

PhotoRec
Web: www.cgsecurity.org/wiki/PhotoRec

PhotoRescue
Web: www.datarescue.com/photorescue

Scalpel
Web: www.digitalforensicssolutions.com/Scalpel

Simple Carver Suite
Web: www.simplecarver.com

Live analysis tools

The following is not a complete list of tools available for live analysis as new tools are frequently being developed. It does, however, encompass the core tools that would be of use. The majority are freely available online, and more information about a specific tool can be found online.

Resources

arp.exe	nslookup.exe
cmd.exe	ntfsinfo.exe
dd.exe	promiscdetect.exe
dir.exe	ps.exe
fport.exe	psfile.exe
handle.exe	pslist.exe
hostname.exe	psloggedon.exe
ipconfig.exe	psservice.exe
md5sum.exe	rootkitrevealer.exe
Mem.exe	route.exe
nbtstat.exe	sha1sum.exe
net.exe	tracert.exe
netstat.exe	whoami.exe

Password cracking tools

AccessData Password Recovery Toolkit®
Web: *www.accessdata.com*

Cain & Abel
Web: *www.oxid.it/cain.html*

John the Ripper
Web: *www.openwall.com/john*

L0phtCrack
Web: *http://l0phtcrack.com*

Ophcrack
Web: *http://sourceforge.net/projects/ophcrack*

RainbowCrack
Web: *http://project-rainbowcrack.com*

Web resources

Assistant Chief Police Officers (ACPO) Good Practice Guide for Computer-Based Electronic Evidence

Resources

A UK guide developed to provide guidelines for law enforcement officers when seizing and undertaking computer-based forensic investigations.

Web: *www.7safe.com/electronic_evidence/ACPO_guidelines_computer_evidence.pdf*

CERT – Software Engineering Institute, Carnegie Mellon University

A website providing information and guidance on incident response and forensics. Publications include:

- First Responder's Guide to Computer Forensics
- Handbook for Computer Security Incident Response Teams

Web: *www.cert.org*

CSO Online – 'The Rise of Anti-Forensics' by Scott Berinato (June 2007)

An interesting article discussing the growing focus upon anti-forensic tools and techniques.

Web: *http://csoonline.com/article/print/221208*

Digital Forensic Research Workshop (DFRWS)

A volunteer organisation focused upon sharing knowledge on digital forensics. They hold an annual conference from which some of the most notable advancements in forensic research are published. The website contains an archive of the conferences and the papers published.

Web: *www.dfrws.org*

ForensicsWiki

A useful resource for defining and describing digital forensics terms. The site is updated regularly and includes links to the latest research findings within the domain.

Web: *www.forensicswiki.org*

Resources

Metasploit Anti-Forensics Project

A website providing news and tools on the topic of anti-forensics.

Web: *http://metasploit.com/research/projects/antiforensics*

NIST Computer Forensics Reference Data Sets (CFReDS) Project

The project has created a number of forensic test cases that can be used to test forensic software and for the training of forensic investigators.

Web: *www.cfreds.nist.gov*

NIST Computer Forensics Tool Testing Project

A project to establish a methodology for testing the reliability of forensic tools. The project has created specifications for what forensic tools should achieve and test scenarios to use to evaluate tools.

Web: *www.cftt.nist.gov*

NIST Computer Security Resource Centre

A website providing links to NIST projects and publications relating to information security. The Incident Response family of publications include:

- SP800-101 – Guidelines on Cell Phone Forensics
- SP800-83 – Guide to Malware Incident Prevention and Handling
- SP800-61 Rev.1 – Computer Security Incident Handling Guide
- SP800-86 – Guide to Integrating Forensic Techniques into Incident Response
- SP800-72 – Guidelines on PDA Forensics

Web: *http://csrc.nist.gov*

NIST National Software Reference Library (NSRL)

Resources

A freely available database of hash values of trusted OS and application files. To be used to eliminate trusted file from forensic investigations.

Web: *www.nsrl.nist.gov*

SANS Institute – Mobile Device Forensics by Andrew Martin

A detailed technical guide to mobile device forensics.

Web: *www.sans.org/reading_room/whitepapers/forensics/mobile_device_for ensics_32888?show=32888.php&cat=forensics*

US Government Accountability Office (GAO) – Public and Private Entities Face Challenges in Addressing Cyber Threats

A 2007 study looking at the challenges in addressing cyber threats. The report includes aspects for forensic investigators.

Web: *www.gao.gov/new.items/d07705.pdf*

ITG RESOURCES

IT Governance Ltd. sources, creates and delivers products and services to meet the real-world, evolving IT governance needs of today's organisations, directors, managers and practitioners. The ITG website (*www.itgovernance.co.uk*) is the international one-stop-shop for corporate and IT governance information, advice, guidance, books, tools, training and consultancy. www.itgovernance.co.uk/computer_forensics.aspx is the information page from our website for computer forensics resources.

Other Websites

Books and tools published by IT Governance Publishing (ITGP) are available from all business booksellers and are also immediately available from the following websites:

www.itgovernance.co.uk/catalog/355 provides information and online purchasing facilities for every currently available book published by ITGP.

www.itgovernanceusa.com is a US$-based website that delivers the full range of IT Governance products to North America, and ships from within the continental US.

www.itgovernanceasia.com provides a selected range of ITGP products specifically for customers in South Asia.

www.27001.com is the IT Governance Ltd. website that deals specifically with information security management, and ships from within the continental US.

Pocket Guides

For full details of the entire range of pocket guides, simply follow the links at *www.itgovernance.co.uk/publishing.aspx*.

Toolkits

ITG's unique range of toolkits includes the IT Governance Framework Toolkit, which contains all the tools and guidance that you will need in order to develop and implement an appropriate IT governance framework for your organisation. Full details can be found at *www.itgovernance.co.uk/products/519*.

ITG Resources

For a free paper on how to use the proprietary Calder-Moir IT Governance Framework, and for a free trial version of the toolkit, see *www.itgovernance.co.uk/calder_moir.aspx*.

There is also a wide range of toolkits to simplify implementation of management systems, such as an ISO/IEC 27001 ISMS or a BS25999 BCMS, and these can all be viewed and purchased online at: *http://www.itgovernance.co.uk/catalog/1*

Best Practice Reports

ITG's range of Best Practice Reports is now at *www.itgovernance.co.uk/best-practice-reports.aspx*. These offer you essential, pertinent, expertly researched information on an increasing number of key issues, including Web 2.0 and Green IT.

Training and Consultancy

IT Governance also offers training and consultancy services across the entire spectrum of disciplines in the information governance arena. Details of training courses can be accessed at *www.itgovernance.co.uk/training.aspx* and descriptions of our consultancy services can be found at *http://www.itgovernance.co.uk/consulting.aspx*.
Why not contact us to see how we could help you and your organisation?

Newsletter

IT governance is one of the hottest topics in business today, not least because it is also the fastest moving, so what better way to keep up than by subscribing to ITG's free monthly newsletter *Sentinel*? It provides monthly updates and resources across the whole spectrum of IT governance subject matter, including risk management, information security, ITIL and IT service management, project governance, compliance and so much more. Subscribe for your free copy at: *www.itgovernance.co.uk/newsletter.aspx*.